It's Just Your Password Dumb Ass

Robert House

COPYRIGHT © 2019 ROBERT HOUSE
All rights reserved.

Copyright Information Page

ISBN: 9781084151468
Imprint: Independently published

It's Just Your Password Dumb Ass

Use "It's Just Your Password Dumb Ass" to keep all your Internet addresses and their Passwords and User ID's. No more frustration when you cannot remember the Password or User ID.
Put relevant information in the Notes block, such as the date your bank credit card needs to be paid.

Space for the name of the company, the web address, two places for account numbers, the user id, the password, phone numbers and contact names.

Are you tired of forgetting the usernames and passwords you created every time you visit a website?

This discrete password journal lets you store your important internet passwords in one convenient place! This password journal has spaces to record the password, website name, username. You know, all the passwords you can't remember. Why do you need this? In the age of the hacker, this password keeper lets you create unique and difficult passwords for each website and log in with ease! Stop writing your passwords down on sticky notes, get this password journal and change your online experience forever!

Use the calendar at the end to list credit card monthly pay dates.

Robert House

CONTENTS

ACKNOWLEDGMENTS

Thanks to my family for helping along this journey in the world of computers. From my Commodore 64 to my updated new laptop.

It's Just Your Password Dumb Ass

A/B

Website Name: _____

Web Address: _____

User Name: _____

Password: _____

Account #: _____

Account #: _____

Contact: _____

Phone: _____

Cell: _____

Website Name: _____

Web Address: _____

User Name: _____

Password: _____

Account #: _____

Account #: _____

Contact: _____

Phone: _____

Cell: _____

A/B

Website Name: _____

Web Address: _____

User Name: _____

Password: _____

Account #: _____

Account #: _____

Contact: _____

Phone: _____

Cell: _____

Website Name: _____

Web Address: _____

User Name: _____

Password: _____

Account #: _____

Account #: _____

Contact: _____

Phone: _____

Cell: _____

A/B

Website Name: _____

Web Address: _____

User Name: _____

Password: _____

Account #: _____

Account #: _____

Contact: _____

Phone: _____

Cell: _____

Website Name: _____

Web Address: _____

User Name: _____

Password: _____

Account #: _____

Account #: _____

Contact: _____

Phone: _____

Cell: _____

A/B

Website Name: _____

Web Address: _____

User Name: _____

Password: _____

Account #: _____

Account #: _____

Contact: _____

Phone: _____

Cell: _____

Website Name: _____

Web Address: _____

User Name: _____

Password: _____

Account #: _____

Account #: _____

Contact: _____

Phone: _____

Cell: _____

A/B

Website Name: _____

Web Address: _____

User Name: _____

Password: _____

Account #: _____

Account #: _____

Contact: _____

Phone: _____

Cell: _____

Website Name: _____

Web Address: _____

User Name: _____

Password: _____

Account #: _____

Account #: _____

Contact: _____

Phone: _____

Cell: _____

A/B

Website Name: _____

Web Address: _____

User Name: _____

Password: _____

Account #: _____

Account #: _____

Contact: _____

Phone: _____

Cell: _____

Website Name: _____

Web Address: _____

User Name: _____

Password: _____

Account #: _____

Account #: _____

Contact: _____

Phone: _____

Cell: _____

A/B

Website Name: _____

Web Address: _____

User Name: _____

Password: _____

Account #: _____

Account #: _____

Contact: _____

Phone: _____

Cell: _____

Website Name: _____

Web Address: _____

User Name: _____

Password: _____

Account #: _____

Account #: _____

Contact: _____

Phone: _____

Cell: _____

A/B

Website Name: _____

Web Address: _____

User Name: _____

Password: _____

Account #: _____

Account #: _____

Contact: _____

Phone: _____

Cell: _____

Website Name: _____

Web Address: _____

User Name: _____

Password: _____

Account #: _____

Account #: _____

Contact: _____

Phone: _____

Cell: _____

A/B

Website Name: _____

Web Address: _____

User Name: _____

Password: _____

Account #: _____

Account #: _____

Contact: _____

Phone: _____

Cell: _____

Website Name: _____

Web Address: _____

User Name: _____

Password: _____

Account #: _____

Account #: _____

Contact: _____

Phone: _____

Cell: _____

A/B

Website Name: _____

Web Address: _____

User Name: _____

Password: _____

Account #: _____   _____

Account #: _____

Contact: _____

Phone: _____

Cell: _____

Website Name: _____

Web Address: _____

User Name: _____

Password: _____

Account #: _____

Account #: _____

Contact: _____

Phone: _____

Cell: _____

A/B

Website Name: _____

Web Address: _____

User Name: _____

Password: _____

Account #: _____

Account #: _____

Contact: _____

Phone: _____

Cell: _____

Website Name: _____

Web Address: _____

User Name: _____

Password: _____

Account #: _____

Account #: _____

Contact: _____

Phone: _____

Cell: _____

A/B

Website Name: _____

Web Address: _____

User Name: _____

Password: _____

Account #: _____

Account #: _____

Contact: _____

Phone: _____

Cell: _____

Website Name: _____

Web Address: _____

User Name: _____

Password: _____

Account #: _____

Account #: _____

Contact: _____

Phone: _____

Cell: _____

C/D

Website Name: _____

Web Address: _____

User Name: _____

Password: _____

Account #: _____

Account #: _____

Contact: _____

Phone: _____

Cell: _____

Website Name: _____

Web Address: _____

User Name: _____

Password: _____

Account #: _____

Account #: _____

Contact: _____

Phone: _____

Cell: _____

C/D

Website Name: _____

Web Address: _____

User Name: _____

Password: _____

Account #: _____

Account #: _____

Contact: _____

Phone: _____

Cell: _____

Website Name: _____

Web Address: _____

User Name: _____

Password: _____

Account #: _____

Account #: _____

Contact: _____

Phone: _____

Cell: _____

C/D

Website Name: _____

Web Address: _____

User Name: _____

Password: _____

Account #: _____

Account #: _____

Contact: _____

Phone: _____

Cell: _____

Website Name: _____

Web Address: _____

User Name: _____

Password: _____

Account #: _____

Account #: _____

Contact: _____

Phone: _____

Cell: _____

C/D

Website Name: _____

Web Address: _____

User Name: _____

Password: _____

Account #: _____

Account #: _____

Contact: _____

Phone: _____

Cell: _____

Website Name: _____

Web Address: _____

User Name: _____

Password: _____

Account #: _____

Account #: _____

Contact: _____

Phone: _____

Cell: _____

C/D

Website Name: _____

Web Address: _____

User Name: _____

Password: _____

Account #: _____

Account #: _____

Contact: _____

Phone: _____

Cell: _____

Website Name: _____

Web Address: _____

User Name: _____

Password: _____

Account #: _____

Account #: _____

Contact: _____

Phone: _____

Cell: _____

C/D

Website Name: _____

Web Address: _____

User Name: _____

Password: _____

Account #: _____

Account #: _____

Contact: _____

Phone: _____

Cell: _____

Website Name: _____

Web Address: _____

User Name: _____

Password: _____

Account #: _____

Account #: _____

Contact: _____

Phone: _____

Cell: _____

C/D

Website Name: _____

Web Address: _____

User Name: _____

Password: _____

Account #: _____

Account #: _____

Contact: _____

Phone: _____

Cell: _____

Website Name: _____

Web Address: _____

User Name: _____

Password: _____

Account #: _____

Account #: _____

Contact: _____

Phone: _____

Cell: _____

C/D

Website Name: _____

Web Address: _____

User Name: _____

Password: _____

Account #: _____

Account #: _____

Contact: _____

Phone: _____

Cell: _____

Website Name: _____

Web Address: _____

User Name: _____

Password: _____

Account #: _____

Account #: _____

Contact: _____

Phone: _____

Cell: _____

C/D

Website Name: _____

Web Address: _____

User Name: _____

Password: _____

Account #: _____

Account #: _____

Contact: _____

Phone: _____

Cell: _____

Website Name: _____

Web Address: _____

User Name: _____

Password: _____

Account #: _____

Account #: _____

Contact: _____

Phone: _____

Cell: _____

C/D

Website Name: _____

Web Address: _____

User Name: _____

Password: _____

Account #: _____

Account #: _____

Contact: _____

Phone: _____

Cell: _____

Website Name: _____

Web Address: _____

User Name: _____

Password: _____

Account #: _____

Account #: _____

Contact: _____

Phone: _____

Cell: _____

C/D

Website Name: _____

Web Address: _____

User Name: _____

Password: _____

Account #: _____

Account #: _____

Contact: _____

Phone: _____

Cell: _____

Website Name: _____

Web Address: _____

User Name: _____

Password: _____

Account #: _____

Account #: _____

Contact: _____

Phone: _____

Cell: _____

C/D

Website Name: _____

Web Address: _____

User Name: _____

Password: _____

Account #: _____

Account #: _____

Contact: _____

Phone: _____

Cell: _____

Website Name: _____

Web Address: _____

User Name: _____

Password: _____

Account #: _____

Account #: _____

Contact: _____

Phone: _____

Cell: _____

C/D

Website Name: _____

Web Address: _____

User Name: _____

Password: _____

Account #: _____

Account #: _____

Contact: _____

Phone: _____

Cell: _____

Website Name: _____

Web Address: _____

User Name: _____

Password: _____

Account #: _____

Account #: _____

Contact: _____

Phone: _____

Cell: _____

E/F

Website Name: _____

Web Address: _____

User Name: _____

Password: _____

Account #: _____

Account #: _____

Contact: _____

Phone: _____

Cell: _____

Website Name: _____

Web Address: _____

User Name: _____

Password: _____

Account #: _____

Account #: _____

Contact: _____

Phone: _____

Cell: _____

E/F

Website Name: _____

Web Address: _____

User Name: _____

Password: _____

Account #: _____

Account #: _____

Contact: _____

Phone: _____

Cell: _____

Website Name: _____

Web Address: _____

User Name: _____

Password: _____

Account #: _____

Account #: _____

Contact: _____

Phone: _____

Cell: _____

E/F

Website Name: _____

Web Address: _____

User Name: _____

Password: _____

Account #: _____

Account #: _____

Contact: _____

Phone: _____

Cell: _____

Website Name: _____

Web Address: _____

User Name: _____

Password: _____

Account #: _____

Account #: _____

Contact: _____

Phone: _____

Cell: _____

E/F

Website Name: _____

Web Address: _____

User Name: _____

Password: _____

Account #: _____

Account #: _____

Contact: _____

Phone: _____

Cell: _____

Website Name: _____

Web Address: _____

User Name: _____

Password: _____

Account #: _____

Account #: _____

Contact: _____

Phone: _____

Cell: _____

E/F

Website Name: _____

Web Address: _____

User Name: _____

Password: _____

Account #: _____

Account #: _____

Contact: _____

Phone: _____

Cell: _____

Website Name: _____

Web Address: _____

User Name: _____

Password: _____

Account #: _____

Account #: _____

Contact: _____

Phone: _____

Cell: _____

E/F

Website Name: _____

Web Address: _____

User Name: _____

Password: _____

Account #: _____

Account #: _____

Contact: _____

Phone: _____

Cell: _____

Website Name: _____

Web Address: _____

User Name: _____

Password: _____

Account #: _____

Account #: _____

Contact: _____

Phone: _____

Cell: _____

E/F

Website Name: _____

Web Address: _____

User Name: _____

Password: _____

Account #: _____

Account #: _____

Contact: _____

Phone: _____

Cell: _____

Website Name: _____

Web Address: _____

User Name: _____

Password: _____

Account #: _____

Account #: _____

Contact: _____

Phone: _____

Cell: _____

E/F

Website Name: _____

Web Address: _____

User Name: _____

Password: _____

Account #: _____

Account #: _____

Contact: _____

Phone: _____

Cell: _____

Website Name: _____

Web Address: _____

User Name: _____

Password: _____

Account #: _____

Account #: _____

Contact: _____

Phone: _____

Cell: _____

E/F

Website Name: _____

Web Address: _____

User Name: _____

Password: _____

Account #: _____

Account #: _____

Contact: _____

Phone: _____

Cell: _____

Website Name: _____

Web Address: _____

User Name: _____

Password: _____

Account #: _____

Account #: _____

Contact: _____

Phone: _____

Cell: _____

E/F

Website Name: _____

Web Address: _____

User Name: _____

Password: _____

Account #: _____

Account #: _____

Contact: _____

Phone: _____

Cell: _____

Website Name: _____

Web Address: _____

User Name: _____

Password: _____

Account #: _____

Account #: _____

Contact: _____

Phone: _____

Cell: _____

E/F

Website Name: _____

Web Address: _____

User Name: _____

Password: _____

Account #: _____

Account #: _____

Contact: _____

Phone: _____

Cell: _____

Website Name: _____

Web Address: _____

User Name: _____

Password: _____

Account #: _____

Account #: _____

Contact: _____

Phone: _____

Cell: _____

E/F

Website Name: _____

Web Address: _____

User Name: _____

Password: _____

Account #: _____

Account #: _____

Contact: _____

Phone: _____

Cell: _____

Website Name: _____

Web Address: _____

User Name: _____

Password: _____

Account #: _____

Account #: _____

Contact: _____

Phone: _____

Cell: _____

G/H

Website Name: _____

Web Address: _____

User Name: _____

Password: _____

Account #: _____

Account #: _____

Contact: _____

Phone: _____

Cell: _____

Website Name: _____

Web Address: _____

User Name: _____

Password: _____

Account #: _____

Account #: _____

Contact: _____

Phone: _____

Cell: _____

G/H

Website Name: _____

Web Address: _____

User Name: _____

Password: _____

Account #: _____

Account #: _____

Contact: _____

Phone: _____

Cell: _____

Website Name: _____

Web Address: _____

User Name: _____

Password: _____

Account #: _____

Account #: _____

Contact: _____

Phone: _____

Cell: _____

G/H

Website Name: _____

Web Address: _____

User Name: _____

Password: _____

Account #: _____

Account #: _____

Contact: _____

Phone: _____

Cell: _____

Website Name: _____

Web Address: _____

User Name: _____

Password: _____

Account #: _____

Account #: _____

Contact: _____

Phone: _____

Cell: _____

G/H

Website Name: _____

Web Address: _____

User Name: _____

Password: _____

Account #: _____

Account #: _____

Contact: _____

Phone: _____

Cell: _____

Website Name: _____

Web Address: _____

User Name: _____

Password: _____

Account #: _____

Account #: _____

Contact: _____

Phone: _____

Cell: _____

G/H

Website Name: _____

Web Address: _____

User Name: _____

Password: _____

Account #: _____

Account #: _____

Contact: _____

Phone: _____

Cell: _____

Website Name: _____

Web Address: _____

User Name: _____

Password: _____

Account #: _____

Account #: _____

Contact: _____

Phone: _____

Cell: _____

G/H

Website Name: _____

Web Address: _____

User Name: _____

Password: _____

Account #: _____

Account #: _____

Contact: _____

Phone: _____

Cell: _____

Website Name: _____

Web Address: _____

User Name: _____

Password: _____

Account #: _____

Account #: _____

Contact: _____

Phone: _____

Cell: _____

G/H

Website Name: _____

Web Address: _____

User Name: _____

Password: _____

Account #: _____

Account #: _____

Contact: _____

Phone: _____

Cell: _____

Website Name: _____

Web Address: _____

User Name: _____

Password: _____

Account #: _____

Account #: _____

Contact: _____

Phone: _____

Cell: _____

G/H

Website Name: _____

Web Address: _____

User Name: _____

Password: _____

Account #: _____

Account #: _____

Contact: _____

Phone: _____

Cell: _____

Website Name: _____

Web Address: _____

User Name: _____

Password: _____

Account #: _____

Account #: _____

Contact: _____

Phone: _____

Cell: _____

G/H

Website Name: _____

Web Address: _____

User Name: _____

Password: _____

Account #: _____

Account #: _____

Contact: _____

Phone: _____

Cell: _____

Website Name: _____

Web Address: _____

User Name: _____

Password: _____

Account #: _____

Account #: _____

Contact: _____

Phone: _____

Cell: _____

G/H

Website Name: _____

Web Address: _____

User Name: _____

Password: _____

Account #: _____

Account #: _____

Contact: _____

Phone: _____

Cell: _____

Website Name: _____

Web Address: _____

User Name: _____

Password: _____

Account #: _____

Account #: _____

Contact: _____

Phone: _____

Cell: _____

G/H

Website Name: _____

Web Address: _____

User Name: _____

Password: _____

Account #: _____

Account #: _____

Contact: _____

Phone: _____

Cell: _____

Website Name: _____

Web Address: _____

User Name: _____

Password: _____

Account #: _____

Account #: _____

Contact: _____

Phone: _____

Cell: _____

G/H

Website Name: _____

Web Address: _____

User Name: _____

Password: _____

Account #: _____

Account #: _____

Contact: _____

Phone: _____

Cell: _____

Website Name: _____

Web Address: _____

User Name: _____

Password: _____

Account #: _____

Account #: _____

Contact: _____

Phone: _____

Cell: _____

I/J

Website Name: _____

Web Address: _____

User Name: _____

Password: _____

Account #: _____

Account #: _____

Contact: _____

Phone: _____

Cell: _____

Website Name: _____

Web Address: _____

User Name: _____

Password: _____

Account #: _____

Account #: _____

Contact: _____

Phone: _____

Cell: _____

I/J

Website Name: _____

Web Address: _____

User Name: _____

Password: _____

Account #: _____

Account #: _____

Contact: _____

Phone: _____

Cell: _____

Website Name: _____

Web Address: _____

User Name: _____

Password: _____

Account #: _____

Account #: _____

Contact: _____

Phone: _____

Cell: _____

I/J

Website Name: _____

Web Address: _____

User Name: _____

Password: _____

Account #: _____

Account #: _____

Contact: _____

Phone: _____

Cell: _____

Website Name: _____

Web Address: _____

User Name: _____

Password: _____

Account #: _____

Account #: _____

Contact: _____

Phone: _____

Cell: _____

I/J

Website Name: _____

Web Address: _____

User Name: _____

Password: _____

Account #: _____

Account #: _____

Contact: _____

Phone: _____

Cell: _____

Website Name: _____

Web Address: _____

User Name: _____

Password: _____

Account #: _____

Account #: _____

Contact: _____

Phone: _____

Cell: _____

I/J

Website Name: _____

Web Address: _____

User Name: _____

Password: _____

Account #: _____

Account #: _____

Contact: _____

Phone: _____

Cell: _____

Website Name: _____

Web Address: _____

User Name: _____

Password: _____

Account #: _____

Account #: _____

Contact: _____

Phone: _____

Cell: _____

I/J

Website Name: _____

Web Address: _____

User Name: _____

Password: _____

Account #: _____

Account #: _____

Contact: _____

Phone: _____

Cell: _____

Website Name: _____

Web Address: _____

User Name: _____

Password: _____

Account #: _____

Account #: _____

Contact: _____

Phone: _____

Cell: _____

I/J

Website Name: _____

Web Address: _____

User Name: _____

Password: _____

Account #: _____

Account #: _____

Contact: _____

Phone: _____

Cell: _____

Website Name: _____

Web Address: _____

User Name: _____

Password: _____

Account #: _____

Account #: _____

Contact: _____

Phone: _____

Cell: _____

I/J

Website Name: _____

Web Address: _____

User Name: _____

Password: _____

Account #: _____

Account #: _____

Contact: _____

Phone: _____

Cell: _____

Website Name: _____

Web Address: _____

User Name: _____

Password: _____

Account #: _____

Account #: _____

Contact: _____

Phone: _____

Cell: _____

I/J

Website Name: _____

Web Address: _____

User Name: _____

Password: _____

Account #: _____

Account #: _____

Contact: _____

Phone: _____

Cell: _____

Website Name: _____

Web Address: _____

User Name: _____

Password: _____

Account #: _____

Account #: _____

Contact: _____

Phone: _____

Cell: _____

I/J

Website Name: _____

Web Address: _____

User Name: _____

Password: _____

Account #: _____

Account #: _____

Contact: _____

Phone: _____

Cell: _____

Website Name: _____

Web Address: _____

User Name: _____

Password: _____

Account #: _____

Account #: _____

Contact: _____

Phone: _____

Cell: _____

I/J

Website Name: _____

Web Address: _____

User Name: _____

Password: _____

Account #: _____

Account #: _____

Contact: _____

Phone: _____

Cell: _____

Website Name: _____

Web Address: _____

User Name: _____

Password: _____

Account #: _____

Account #: _____

Contact: _____

Phone: _____

Cell: _____

I/J

Website Name: _____

Web Address: _____

User Name: _____

Password: _____

Account #: _____

Account #: _____

Contact: _____

Phone: _____

Cell: _____

Website Name: _____

Web Address: _____

User Name: _____

Password: _____

Account #: _____

Account #: _____

Contact: _____

Phone: _____

Cell: _____

I/J

Website Name: _____

Web Address: _____

User Name: _____

Password: _____

Account #: _____

Account #: _____

Contact: _____

Phone: _____

Cell: _____

Website Name: _____

Web Address: _____

User Name: _____

Password: _____

Account #: _____

Account #: _____

Contact: _____

Phone: _____

Cell: _____

K/L

Website Name: _____

Web Address: _____

User Name: _____

Password: _____

Account #: _____

Account #: _____

Contact: _____

Phone: _____

Cell: _____

Website Name: _____

Web Address: _____

User Name: _____

Password: _____

Account #: _____

Account #: _____

Contact: _____

Phone: _____

Cell: _____

K/L

Website Name: _____

Web Address: _____

User Name: _____

Password: _____

Account #: _____

Account #: _____

Contact: _____

Phone: _____

Cell: _____

Website Name: _____

Web Address: _____

User Name: _____

Password: _____

Account #: _____

Account #: _____

Contact: _____

Phone: _____

Cell: _____

K/L

Website Name: _____

Web Address: _____

User Name: _____

Password: _____

Account #: _____

Account #: _____

Contact: _____

Phone: _____

Cell: _____

Website Name: _____

Web Address: _____

User Name: _____

Password: _____

Account #: _____

Account #: _____

Contact: _____

Phone: _____

Cell: _____

K/L

Website Name: _____

Web Address: _____

User Name: _____

Password: _____

Account #: _____

Account #: _____

Contact: _____

Phone: _____

Cell: _____

Website Name: _____

Web Address: _____

User Name: _____

Password: _____

Account #: _____

Account #: _____

Contact: _____

Phone: _____

Cell: _____

K/L

Website Name: _____

Web Address: _____

User Name: _____

Password: _____

Account #: _____

Account #: _____

Contact: _____

Phone: _____

Cell: _____

Website Name: _____

Web Address: _____

User Name: _____

Password: _____

Account #: _____

Account #: _____

Contact: _____

Phone: _____

Cell: _____

K/L

Website Name: _____

Web Address: _____

User Name: _____

Password: _____

Account #: _____

Account #: _____

Contact: _____

Phone: _____

Cell: _____

Website Name: _____

Web Address: _____

User Name: _____

Password: _____

Account #: _____

Account #: _____

Contact: _____

Phone: _____

Cell: _____

K/L

Website Name: _____

Web Address: _____

User Name: _____

Password: _____

Account #: _____

Account #: _____

Contact: _____

Phone: _____

Cell: _____

Website Name: _____

Web Address: _____

User Name: _____

Password: _____

Account #: _____

Account #: _____

Contact: _____

Phone: _____

Cell: _____

K/L

Website Name: _____

Web Address: _____

User Name: _____

Password: _____

Account #: _____

Account #: _____

Contact: _____

Phone: _____

Cell: _____

Website Name: _____

Web Address: _____

User Name: _____

Password: _____

Account #: _____

Account #: _____

Contact: _____

Phone: _____

Cell: _____

K/L

Website Name: _____

Web Address: _____

User Name: _____

Password: _____

Account #: _____

Account #: _____

Contact: _____

Phone: _____

Cell: _____

Website Name: _____

Web Address: _____

User Name: _____

Password: _____

Account #: _____

Account #: _____

Contact: _____

Phone: _____

Cell: _____

K/L

Website Name: _____

Web Address: _____

User Name: _____

Password: _____

Account #: _____

Account #: _____

Contact: _____

Phone: _____

Cell: _____

Website Name: _____

Web Address: _____

User Name: _____

Password: _____

Account #: _____

Account #: _____

Contact: _____

Phone: _____

Cell: _____

K/L

Website Name: _____

Web Address: _____

User Name: _____

Password: _____

Account #: _____

Account #: _____

Contact: _____

Phone: _____

Cell: _____

Website Name: _____

Web Address: _____

User Name: _____

Password: _____

Account #: _____

Account #: _____

Contact: _____

Phone: _____

Cell: _____

K/L

Website Name: _____

Web Address: _____

User Name: _____

Password: _____

Account #: _____

Account #: _____

Contact: _____

Phone: _____

Cell: _____

Website Name: _____

Web Address: _____

User Name: _____

Password: _____

Account #: _____

Account #: _____

Contact: _____

Phone: _____

Cell: _____

M/N

Website Name: _____

Web Address: _____

User Name: _____

Password: _____

Account #: _____

Account #: _____

Contact: _____

Phone: _____

Cell: _____

Website Name: _____

Web Address: _____

User Name: _____

Password: _____

Account #: _____

Account #: _____

Contact: _____

Phone: _____

Cell: _____

M/N

Website Name: _____

Web Address: _____

User Name: _____

Password: _____

Account #: _____

Account #: _____

Contact: _____

Phone: _____

Cell: _____

Website Name: _____

Web Address: _____

User Name: _____

Password: _____

Account #: _____

Account #: _____

Contact: _____

Phone: _____

Cell: _____

M/N

Website Name: _____

Web Address: _____

User Name: _____

Password: _____

Account #: _____

Account #: _____

Contact: _____

Phone: _____

Cell: _____

Website Name: _____

Web Address: _____

User Name: _____

Password: _____

Account #: _____

Account #: _____

Contact: _____

Phone: _____

Cell: _____

M/N

Website Name: _____

Web Address: _____

User Name: _____

Password: _____

Account #: _____

Account #: _____

Contact: _____

Phone: _____

Cell: _____

Website Name: _____

Web Address: _____

User Name: _____

Password: _____

Account #: _____

Account #: _____

Contact: _____

Phone: _____

Cell: _____

M/N

Website Name: _____

Web Address: _____

User Name: _____

Password: _____

Account #: _____

Account #: _____

Contact: _____

Phone: _____

Cell: _____

Website Name: _____

Web Address: _____

User Name: _____

Password: _____

Account #: _____

Account #: _____

Contact: _____

Phone: _____

Cell: _____

M/N

Website Name: _____

Web Address: _____

User Name: _____

Password: _____

Account #: _____

Account #: _____

Contact: _____

Phone: _____

Cell: _____

Website Name: _____

Web Address: _____

User Name: _____

Password: _____

Account #: _____

Account #: _____

Contact: _____

Phone: _____

Cell: _____

M/N

Website Name: _____

Web Address: _____

User Name: _____

Password: _____

Account #: _____

Account #: _____

Contact: _____

Phone: _____

Cell: _____

Website Name: _____

Web Address: _____

User Name: _____

Password: _____

Account #: _____

Account #: _____

Contact: _____

Phone: _____

Cell: _____

M/N

Website Name: _____

Web Address: _____

User Name: _____

Password: _____

Account #: _____

Account #: _____

Contact: _____

Phone: _____

Cell: _____

Website Name: _____

Web Address: _____

User Name: _____

Password: _____

Account #: _____

Account #: _____

Contact: _____

Phone: _____

Cell: _____

M/N

Website Name: _____

Web Address: _____

User Name: _____

Password: _____

Account #: _____

Account #: _____

Contact: _____

Phone: _____

Cell: _____

Website Name: _____

Web Address: _____

User Name: _____

Password: _____

Account #: _____

Account #: _____

Contact: _____

Phone: _____

Cell: _____

M/N

Website Name: _____

Web Address: _____

User Name: _____

Password: _____

Account #: _____

Account #: _____

Contact: _____

Phone: _____

Cell: _____

Website Name: _____

Web Address: _____

User Name: _____

Password: _____

Account #: _____

Account #: _____

Contact: _____

Phone: _____

Cell: _____

M/N

Website Name: _____

Web Address: _____

User Name: _____

Password: _____

Account #: _____

Account #: _____

Contact: _____

Phone: _____

Cell: _____

Website Name: _____

Web Address: _____

User Name: _____

Password: _____

Account #: _____

Account #: _____

Contact: _____

Phone: _____

Cell: _____

M/N

Website Name: _____

Web Address: _____

User Name: _____

Password: _____

Account #: _____

Account #: _____

Contact: _____

Phone: _____

Cell: _____

Website Name: _____

Web Address: _____

User Name: _____

Password: _____

Account #: _____

Account #: _____

Contact: _____

Phone: _____

Cell: _____

O/P

Website Name: _____

Web Address: _____

User Name: _____

Password: _____

Account #: _____

Account #: _____

Contact: _____

Phone: _____

Cell: _____

Website Name: _____

Web Address: _____

User Name: _____

Password: _____

Account #: _____

Account #: _____

Contact: _____

Phone: _____

Cell: _____

O/P

Website Name: _____

Web Address: _____

User Name: _____

Password: _____

Account #: _____

Account #: _____

Contact: _____

Phone: _____

Cell: _____

Website Name: _____

Web Address: _____

User Name: _____

Password: _____

Account #: _____

Account #: _____

Contact: _____

Phone: _____

Cell: _____

O/P

Website Name: _____

Web Address: _____

User Name: _____

Password: _____

Account #: _____

Account #: _____

Contact: _____

Phone: _____

Cell: _____

Website Name: _____

Web Address: _____

User Name: _____

Password: _____

Account #: _____

Account #: _____

Contact: _____

Phone: _____

Cell: _____

O/P

Website Name: _____

Web Address: _____

User Name: _____

Password: _____

Account #: _____

Account #: _____

Contact: _____

Phone: _____

Cell: _____

Website Name: _____

Web Address: _____

User Name: _____

Password: _____

Account #: _____

Account #: _____

Contact: _____

Phone: _____

Cell: _____

O/P

Website Name: _____

Web Address: _____

User Name: _____

Password: _____

Account #: _____

Account #: _____

Contact: _____

Phone: _____

Cell: _____

Website Name: _____

Web Address: _____

User Name: _____

Password: _____

Account #: _____

Account #: _____

Contact: _____

Phone: _____

Cell: _____

O/P

Website Name: _____

Web Address: _____

User Name: _____

Password: _____

Account #: _____

Account #: _____

Contact: _____

Phone: _____

Cell: _____

Website Name: _____

Web Address: _____

User Name: _____

Password: _____

Account #: _____

Account #: _____

Contact: _____

Phone: _____

Cell: _____

O/P

Website Name: _____

Web Address: _____

User Name: _____

Password: _____

Account #: _____

Account #: _____

Contact: _____

Phone: _____

Cell: _____

Website Name: _____

Web Address: _____

User Name: _____

Password: _____

Account #: _____

Account #: _____

Contact: _____

Phone: _____

Cell: _____

O/P

Website Name: _____

Web Address: _____

User Name: _____

Password: _____

Account #: _____

Account #: _____

Contact: _____

Phone: _____

Cell: _____

Website Name: _____

Web Address: _____

User Name: _____

Password: _____

Account #: _____

Account #: _____

Contact: _____

Phone: _____

Cell: _____

O/P

Website Name: _____

Web Address: _____

User Name: _____

Password: _____

Account #: _____

Account #: _____

Contact: _____

Phone: _____

Cell: _____

Website Name: _____

Web Address: _____

User Name: _____

Password: _____

Account #: _____

Account #: _____

Contact: _____

Phone: _____

Cell: _____

O/P

Website Name: _____

Web Address: _____

User Name: _____

Password: _____

Account #: _____

Account #: _____

Contact: _____

Phone: _____

Cell: _____

Website Name: _____

Web Address: _____

User Name: _____

Password: _____

Account #: _____

Account #: _____

Contact: _____

Phone: _____

Cell: _____

O/P

Website Name: _____

Web Address: _____

User Name: _____

Password: _____

Account #: _____

Account #: _____

Contact: _____

Phone: _____

Cell: _____

Website Name: _____

Web Address: _____

User Name: _____

Password: _____

Account #: _____

Account #: _____

Contact: _____

Phone: _____

Cell: _____

O/P

Website Name: _____

Web Address: _____

User Name: _____

Password: _____

Account #: _____

Account #: _____

Contact: _____

Phone: _____

Cell: _____

Website Name: _____

Web Address: _____

User Name: _____

Password: _____

Account #: _____

Account #: _____

Contact: _____

Phone: _____

Cell: _____

Q/R

Website Name: _____

Web Address: _____

User Name: _____

Password: _____

Account #: _____

Account #: _____

Contact: _____

Phone: _____

Cell: _____

Website Name: _____

Web Address: _____

User Name: _____

Password: _____

Account #: _____

Account #: _____

Contact: _____

Phone: _____

Cell: _____

Q/R

Website Name: _____

Web Address: _____

User Name: _____

Password: _____

Account #: _____

Account #: _____

Contact: _____

Phone: _____

Cell: _____

Website Name: _____

Web Address: _____

User Name: _____

Password: _____

Account #: _____

Account #: _____

Contact: _____

Phone: _____

Cell: _____

Q/R

Website Name: _____

Web Address: _____

User Name: _____

Password: _____

Account #: _____

Account #: _____

Contact: _____

Phone: _____

Cell: _____

Website Name: _____

Web Address: _____

User Name: _____

Password: _____

Account #: _____

Account #: _____

Contact: _____

Phone: _____

Cell: _____

Q/R

Website Name: _____

Web Address: _____

User Name: _____

Password: _____

Account #: _____

Account #: _____

Contact: _____

Phone: _____

Cell: _____

Website Name: _____

Web Address: _____

User Name: _____

Password: _____

Account #: _____

Account #: _____

Contact: _____

Phone: _____

CELL: _____

Q/R

Website Name: _____

Web Address: _____

User Name: _____

Password: _____

Account #: _____

Account #: _____

Contact: _____

Phone: _____

Cell: _____

Website Name: _____

Web Address: _____

User Name: _____

Password: _____

Account #: _____

Account #: _____

Contact: _____

Phone: _____

CELL: _____

Q/R

Website Name: _____

Web Address: _____

User Name: _____

Password: _____

Account #: _____

Account #: _____

Contact: _____

Phone: _____

Cell: _____

Website Name: _____

Web Address: _____

User Name: _____

Password: _____

Account #: _____

Account #: _____

Contact: _____

Phone: _____

CELL: _____

Q/R

Website Name: _____

Web Address: _____

User Name: _____

Password: _____

Account #: _____

Account #: _____

Contact: _____

Phone: _____

Cell: _____

Website Name: _____

Web Address: _____

User Name: _____

Password: _____

Account #: _____

Account #: _____

Contact: _____

Phone: _____

CELL: _____

Q/R

Website Name: _____

Web Address: _____

User Name: _____

Password: _____

Account #: _____

Account #: _____

Contact: _____

Phone: _____

Cell: _____

Website Name: _____

Web Address: _____

User Name: _____

Password: _____

Account #: _____

Account #: _____

Contact: _____

Phone: _____

CELL: _____

Q/R

Website Name: _____

Web Address: _____

User Name: _____

Password: _____

Account #: _____

Account #: _____

Contact: _____

Phone: _____

Cell: _____

Website Name: _____

Web Address: _____

User Name: _____

Password: _____

Account #: _____

Account #: _____

Contact: _____

Phone: _____

CELL: _____

Q/R

Website Name: _____

Web Address: _____

User Name: _____

Password: _____

Account #: _____

Account #: _____

Contact: _____

Phone: _____

Cell: _____

Website Name: _____

Web Address: _____

User Name: _____

Password: _____

Account #: _____

Account #: _____

Contact: _____

Phone: _____

CELL: _____

Q/R

Website Name: _____

Web Address: _____

User Name: _____

Password: _____

Account #: _____

Account #: _____

Contact: _____

Phone: _____

Cell: _____

Website Name: _____

Web Address: _____

User Name: _____

Password: _____

Account #: _____

Account #: _____

Contact: _____

Phone: _____

CELL: _____

Q/R

Website Name: _____

Web Address: _____

User Name: _____

Password: _____

Account #: _____

Account #: _____

Contact: _____

Phone: _____

Cell: _____

Website Name: _____

Web Address: _____

User Name: _____

Password: _____

Account #: _____

Account #: _____

Contact: _____

Phone: _____

CELL: _____

S/T

Website Name: _____

Web Address: _____

User Name: _____

Password: _____

Account #: _____

Account #: _____

Contact: _____

Phone: _____

Cell: _____

Website Name: _____

Web Address: _____

User Name: _____

Password: _____

Account #: _____

Account #: _____

Contact: _____

Phone: _____

Cell: _____

S/T

Website Name: _____

Web Address: _____

User Name: _____

Password: _____

Account #: _____

Account #: _____

Contact: _____

Phone: _____

Cell: _____

Website Name: _____

Web Address: _____

User Name: _____

Password: _____

Account #: _____

Account #: _____

Contact: _____

Phone: _____

Cell: _____

S/T

Website Name: _____

Web Address: _____

User Name: _____

Password: _____

Account #: _____

Account #: _____

Contact: _____

Phone: _____

Cell: _____

Website Name: _____

Web Address: _____

User Name: _____

Password: _____

Account #: _____

Account #: _____

Contact: _____

Phone: _____

Cell: _____

S/T

Website Name: _____

Web Address: _____

User Name: _____

Password: _____

Account #: _____

Account #: _____

Contact: _____

Phone: _____

Cell: _____

Website Name: _____

Web Address: _____

User Name: _____

Password: _____

Account #: _____

Account #: _____

Contact: _____

Phone: _____

CELL: _____

S/T

Website Name: _____

Web Address: _____

User Name: _____

Password: _____

Account #: _____

Account #: _____

Contact: _____

Phone: _____

Cell: _____

Website Name: _____

Web Address: _____

User Name: _____

Password: _____

Account #: _____

Account #: _____

Contact: _____

Phone: _____

CELL: _____

S/T

Website Name: _____

Web Address: _____

User Name: _____

Password: _____

Account #: _____

Account #: _____

Contact: _____

Phone: _____

Cell: _____

Website Name: _____

Web Address: _____

User Name: _____

Password: _____

Account #: _____

Account #: _____

Contact: _____

Phone: _____

CELL: _____

S/T

Website Name: _____

Web Address: _____

User Name: _____

Password: _____

Account #: _____

Account #: _____

Contact: _____

Phone: _____

Cell: _____

Website Name: _____

Web Address: _____

User Name: _____

Password: _____

Account #: _____

Account #: _____

Contact: _____

Phone: _____

CELL: _____

S/T

Website Name: _____

Web Address: _____

User Name: _____

Password: _____

Account #: _____

Account #: _____

Contact: _____

Phone: _____

Cell: _____

Website Name: _____

Web Address: _____

User Name: _____

Password: _____

Account #: _____

Account #: _____

Contact: _____

Phone: _____

CELL: _____

S/T

Website Name: _____

Web Address: _____

User Name: _____

Password: _____

Account #: _____

Account #: _____

Contact: _____

Phone: _____

Cell: _____

Website Name: _____

Web Address: _____

User Name: _____

Password: _____

Account #: _____

Account #: _____

Contact: _____

Phone: _____

CELL: _____

S/T

Website Name: _____

Web Address: _____

User Name: _____

Password: _____

Account #: _____

Account #: _____

Contact: _____

Phone: _____

Cell: _____

Website Name: _____

Web Address: _____

User Name: _____

Password: _____

Account #: _____

Account #: _____

Contact: _____

Phone: _____

CELL: _____

S/T

Website Name: _____

Web Address: _____

User Name: _____

Password: _____

Account #: _____

Account #: _____

Contact: _____

Phone: _____

Cell: _____

Website Name: _____

Web Address: _____

User Name: _____

Password: _____

Account #: _____

Account #: _____

Contact: _____

Phone: _____

CELL: _____

S/T

Website Name: _____

Web Address: _____

User Name: _____

Password: _____

Account #: _____

Account #: _____

Contact: _____

Phone: _____

Cell: _____

Website Name: _____

Web Address: _____

User Name: _____

Password: _____

Account #: _____

Account #: _____

Contact: _____

Phone: _____

CELL: _____

U/V

Website Name: _____

Web Address: _____

User Name: _____

Password: _____

Account #: _____

Account #: _____

Contact: _____

Phone: _____

Cell: _____

Website Name: _____

Web Address: _____

User Name: _____

Password: _____

Account #: _____

Account #: _____

Contact: _____

Phone: _____

CELL: _____

U/V

Website Name: _____

Web Address: _____

User Name: _____

Password: _____

Account #: _____

Account #: _____

Contact: _____

Phone: _____

Cell: _____

Website Name: _____

Web Address: _____

User Name: _____

Password: _____

Account #: _____

Account #: _____

Contact: _____

Phone: _____

Cell: _____

U/V

Website Name: _____

Web Address: _____

User Name: _____

Password: _____

Account #: _____

Account #: _____

Contact: _____

Phone: _____

Cell: _____

Website Name: _____

Web Address: _____

User Name: _____

Password: _____

Account #: _____

Account #: _____

Contact: _____

Phone: _____

Cell: _____

U/V

Website Name: _____

Web Address: _____

User Name: _____

Password: _____

Account #: _____

Account #: _____

Contact: _____

Phone: _____

Cell: _____

Website Name: _____

Web Address: _____

User Name: _____

Password: _____

Account #: _____

Account #: _____

Contact: _____

Phone: _____

CELL: _____

U/V

Website Name: _____

Web Address: _____

User Name: _____

Password: _____

Account #: _____

Account #: _____

Contact: _____

Phone: _____

Cell: _____

Website Name: _____

Web Address: _____

User Name: _____

Password: _____

Account #: _____

Account #: _____

Contact: _____

Phone: _____

CELL: _____

U/V

Website Name: _____

Web Address: _____

User Name: _____

Password: _____

Account #: _____

Account #: _____

Contact: _____

Phone: _____

Cell: _____

Website Name: _____

Web Address: _____

User Name: _____

Password: _____

Account #: _____

Account #: _____

Contact: _____

Phone: _____

CELL: _____

U/V

Website Name: _____

Web Address: _____

User Name: _____

Password: _____

Account #: _____

Account #: _____

Contact: _____

Phone: _____

Cell: _____

Website Name: _____

Web Address: _____

User Name: _____

Password: _____

Account #: _____

Account #: _____

Contact: _____

Phone: _____

CELL: _____

U/V

Website Name: _____

Web Address: _____

User Name: _____

Password: _____

Account #: _____

Account #: _____

Contact: _____

Phone: _____

Cell: _____

Website Name: _____

Web Address: _____

User Name: _____

Password: _____

Account #: _____

Account #: _____

Contact: _____

Phone: _____

CELL: _____

U/V

Website Name: _____

Web Address: _____

User Name: _____

Password: _____

Account #: _____

Account #: _____

Contact: _____

Phone: _____

Cell: _____

Website Name: _____

Web Address: _____

User Name: _____

Password: _____

Account #: _____

Account #: _____

Contact: _____

Phone: _____

CELL: _____

U/V

Website Name: _____

Web Address: _____

User Name: _____

Password: _____

Account #: _____

Account #: _____

Contact: _____

Phone: _____

Cell: _____

Website Name: _____

Web Address: _____

User Name: _____

Password: _____

Account #: _____

Account #: _____

Contact: _____

Phone: _____

CELL: _____

U/V

Website Name: _____

Web Address: _____

User Name: _____

Password: _____

Account #: _____

Account #: _____

Contact: _____

Phone: _____

Cell: _____

Website Name: _____

Web Address: _____

User Name: _____

Password: _____

Account #: _____

Account #: _____

Contact: _____

Phone: _____

CELL: _____

U/V

Website Name: _____

Web Address: _____

User Name: _____

Password: _____

Account #: _____

Account #: _____

Contact: _____

Phone: _____

Cell: _____

Website Name: _____

Web Address: _____

User Name: _____

Password: _____

Account #: _____

Account #: _____

Contact: _____

Phone: _____

CELL: _____

W/X

Website Name: _____

Web Address: _____

User Name: _____

Password: _____

Account #: _____

Account #: _____

Contact: _____

Phone: _____

Cell: _____

Website Name: _____

Web Address: _____

User Name: _____

Password: _____

Account #: _____

Account #: _____

Contact: _____

Phone: _____

CELL: _____

W/X

Website Name: _____

Web Address: _____

User Name: _____

Password: _____

Account #: _____

Account #: _____

Contact: _____

Phone: _____

Cell: _____

Website Name: _____

Web Address: _____

User Name: _____

Password: _____

Account #: _____

Account #: _____

Contact: _____

Phone: _____

CELL: _____

W/X

Website Name: _____

Web Address: _____

User Name: _____

Password: _____

Account #: _____

Account #: _____

Contact: _____

Phone: _____

Cell: _____

Website Name: _____

Web Address: _____

User Name: _____

Password: _____

Account #: _____

Account #: _____

Contact: _____

Phone: _____

CELL: _____

W/X

Website Name: _____

Web Address: _____

User Name: _____

Password: _____

Account #: _____

Account #: _____

Contact: _____

Phone: _____

Cell: _____

Website Name: _____

Web Address: _____

User Name: _____

Password: _____

Account #: _____

Account #: _____

Contact: _____

Phone: _____

CELL: _____

W/X

Website Name: _____

Web Address: _____

User Name: _____

Password: _____

Account #: _____

Account #: _____

Contact: _____

Phone: _____

Cell: _____

Website Name: _____

Web Address: _____

User Name: _____

Password: _____

Account #: _____

Account #: _____

Contact: _____

Phone: _____

CELL: _____

W/X

Website Name: _____

Web Address: _____

User Name: _____

Password: _____

Account #: _____

Account #: _____

Contact: _____

Phone: _____

Cell: _____

Website Name: _____

Web Address: _____

User Name: _____

Password: _____

Account #: _____

Account #: _____

Contact: _____

Phone: _____

CELL: _____

W/X

Website Name: _____

Web Address: _____

User Name: _____

Password: _____

Account #: _____

Account #: _____

Contact: _____

Phone: _____

Cell: _____

Website Name: _____

Web Address: _____

User Name: _____

Password: _____

Account #: _____

Account #: _____

Contact: _____

Phone: _____

CELL: _____

W/X

Website Name: _____

Web Address: _____

User Name: _____

Password: _____

Account #: _____

Account #: _____

Contact: _____

Phone: _____

Cell: _____

Website Name: _____

Web Address: _____

User Name: _____

Password: _____

Account #: _____

Account #: _____

Contact: _____

Phone: _____

CELL: _____

W/X

Website Name: _____

Web Address: _____

User Name: _____

Password: _____

Account #: _____

Account #: _____

Contact: _____

Phone: _____

Cell: _____

Website Name: _____

Web Address: _____

User Name: _____

Password: _____

Account #: _____

Account #: _____

Contact: _____

Phone: _____

CELL: _____

W/X

Website Name: _____

Web Address: _____

User Name: _____

Password: _____

Account #: _____

Account #: _____

Contact: _____

Phone: _____

Cell: _____

Website Name: _____

Web Address: _____

User Name: _____

Password: _____

Account #: _____

Account #: _____

Contact: _____

Phone: _____

CELL: _____

W/X

Website Name: _____

Web Address: _____

User Name: _____

Password: _____

Account #: _____

Account #: _____

Contact: _____

Phone: _____

Cell: _____

Website Name: _____

Web Address: _____

User Name: _____

Password: _____

Account #: _____

Account #: _____

Contact: _____

Phone: _____

CELL: _____

W/X

Website Name: _____

Web Address: _____

User Name: _____

Password: _____

Account #: _____

Account #: _____

Contact: _____

Phone: _____

Cell: _____

Website Name: _____

Web Address: _____

User Name: _____

Password: _____

Account #: _____

Account #: _____

Contact: _____

Phone: _____

CELL: _____

Y/Z

Website Name: _____

Web Address: _____

User Name: _____

Password: _____

Account #: _____

Account #: _____

Contact: _____

Phone: _____

Cell: _____

Website Name: _____

Web Address: _____

User Name: _____

Password: _____

Account #: _____

Account #: _____

Contact: _____

Phone: _____

CELL: _____

Y/Z

Website Name: _____

Web Address: _____

User Name: _____

Password: _____

Account #: _____

Account #: _____

Contact: _____

Phone: _____

Cell: _____

Website Name: _____

Web Address: _____

User Name: _____

Password: _____

Account #: _____

Account #: _____

Contact: _____

Phone: _____

CELL: _____

Y/Z

Website Name: _____

Web Address: _____

User Name: _____

Password: _____

Account #: _____

Account #: _____

Contact: _____

Phone: _____

Cell: _____

Website Name: _____

Web Address: _____

User Name: _____

Password: _____

Account #: _____

Account #: _____

Contact: _____

Phone: _____

CELL: _____

Y/Z

Website Name: _____

Web Address: _____

User Name: _____

Password: _____

Account #: _____

Account #: _____

Contact: _____

Phone: _____

Cell: _____

Website Name: _____

Web Address: _____

User Name: _____

Password: _____

Account #: _____

Account #: _____

Contact: _____

Phone: _____

CELL: _____

Y/Z

Website Name: _____

Web Address: _____

User Name: _____

Password: _____

Account #: _____

Account #: _____

Contact: _____

Phone: _____

Cell: _____

Website Name: _____

Web Address: _____

User Name: _____

Password: _____

Account #: _____

Account #: _____

Contact: _____

Phone: _____

CELL: _____

Y/Z

Website Name: _____

Web Address: _____

User Name: _____

Password: _____

Account #: _____

Account #: _____

Contact: _____

Phone: _____

Cell: _____

Website Name: _____

Web Address: _____

User Name: _____

Password: _____

Account #: _____

Account #: _____

Contact: _____

Phone: _____

CELL: _____

Y/Z

Website Name: _____

Web Address: _____

User Name: _____

Password: _____

Account #: _____

Account #: _____

Contact: _____

Phone: _____

Cell: _____

Website Name: _____

Web Address: _____

User Name: _____

Password: _____

Account #: _____

Account #: _____

Contact: _____

Phone: _____

CELL: _____

Y/Z

Website Name: _____

Web Address: _____

User Name: _____

Password: _____

Account #: _____

Account #: _____

Contact: _____

Phone: _____

Cell: _____

Website Name: _____

Web Address: _____

User Name: _____

Password: _____

Account #: _____

Account #: _____

Contact: _____

Phone: _____

CELL: _____

Y/Z

Website Name: _____

Web Address: _____

User Name: _____

Password: _____

Account #: _____

Account #: _____

Contact: _____

Phone: _____

Cell: _____

Website Name: _____

Web Address: _____

User Name: _____

Password: _____

Account #: _____

Account #: _____

Contact: _____

Phone: _____

CELL: _____

Y/Z

Website Name: _____

Web Address: _____

User Name: _____

Password: _____

Account #: _____

Account #: _____

Contact: _____

Phone: _____

Cell: _____

Website Name: _____

Web Address: _____

User Name: _____

Password: _____

Account #: _____

Account #: _____

Contact: _____

Phone: _____

CELL: _____

A Reminder for Your Monthly Bills

MONTHLY BILLS						
	1	2	3	4	5	6
7	8	9	10	11	12	13
14	15	16	17	18	19	20
21	22	23	24	25	26	27
28	29	30	31	Notes:		

A Reminder for Your Monthly Bills

MONTHLY BILLS						
	1	2	3	4	5	6
7	8	9	10	11	12	13
14	15	16	17	18	19	20
21	22	23	24	25	26	27
28	29	30	31	Notes:		

ABOUT THE AUTHOR

Robert House has helped a number of authors their book published on particularly the Kindle platform. He is currently working on several projects.

www.ingramcontent.com/pod-product-compliance
Lightning Source LLC
Chambersburg PA
CBHW031220050326
40689CB00009B/1415